Mum has said that Tom and Bella can paint at the kitchen table.

She has given them some paper, two paint boxes, two brushes and two water pots.

But, she bangs her pot of water.
It tips up. Water goes all over
her garden full of flowers.

'If you do something bad, Bella, something bad will happen to you,' says Tom.